eBay Newbie

How to Make Your First Thousand Dollars on eBay

Copyright © 2014 / 2017 Nick Vulich

Contact me at

E-mail: hi@nickvulich.com
Blog: indieauthorstoolbox.com

Amazon Author Page:

- amazon.com/author/nickvulich

Why you should read this book

One thing I've discovered after fourteen years of selling on eBay is the market is always changing. Just when you think you've got it figured out, either eBay comes along and changes the rules of the game, or the economy changes, and your niche implodes, sending your sales straight down the toilet.

One of the biggest things you're going to have to deal with is eBay's constant string of changes. As I'm writing this, eBay has just announced their summer changes, and let me tell you – the entire year has been a crazy roller coaster ride for eBay sellers.

The 2017 Summer Seller Update raised Store subscription fees for most sellers.

Here's the reality.

Basic Store

- Fees range from $19.95 to $24.95 per month
- 250 free listings (fixed price)
- 250 free listings (auction style)
- 20 cents for each fixed price listing
- 25 cents for each auction listing
- Final value (3.5 – 9 percent of final value)

Premium store

- Fees range from $59.95 to $74.95 per month
- 1,000 free listings (fixed price)
- 500 free listings (auction style)
- 10 cents for each fixed price listing
- 15 cents for each auction listing
- Final value (3.5 – 9 percent of final value)

Anchor Store

- Fees range from $299.95 to $349.95 per month
- 10,000 free listings (fixed price)
- 1,000 free listings (auction style)
- 5 cents for each fixed price listing
- 10 cents for each auction listing
- Final value (3.5 – 9 percent of final value)

The good news is – there are no crazy changes on the horizon for sellers with this one. If you haven't checked it out yet, follow this link to read more:

http://pages.ebay.com/seller-center/stores/subscriptions.html

Here are the highlights from that update:

- Buyers and sellers can only communicate using eBay. By September, all contact information needs to be removed from listings. That means phones, fax numbers, email addresses, and street addresses. The same goes for social media links. They are no longer allowed on site.

- Beginning in September, only limited links will be allowed in listings and other eBay pages. Approved links include those to product reviews and installation information, freight shipping information, and legal disclaimers. To view the full list of approved links, follow this link. Pages.ebay.com/help/policies/listings-links.html

- Return policies are changing again. Beginning in the fall, eBay is going to increase exposure of listings that offer "free returns and 30-day or 60-day returns without restocking fees." eBay says it's going to do this by allowing buyers to search for these return policies, highlighting return policies when visitors view your listings and featuring the policy in advertisements. What that means, is if you don't offer extended free returns, it's going to be harder to find your items.

- International performance standards have been updated. Seller performance outside of the United States, Germany, and the United Kingdom will reflect only out of country sales. The idea is buyers from outside of your country can base their choices on how well you perform internationally, independent of your domestic performance. This section does not take full effect until February 20, 2018.

- As always, categories are updating and changing. Sellers need to ensure that their items get listed in the "best fit" category.

Sellers also need to understand the Fall 2016 Update.

Traditionally, eBay releases two seller-updates every year—one in the spring, and another in the fall. These updates are eBay's way of giving seller's a heads-up to let them know what's coming down the pipeline and the changes they need to prepare for.
   Here's a quick run-down of what sellers can expect from the **2016 Fall Seller Update.**

- Active content is prohibited from the site beginning in June of 2016. That means no more videos or animations are allowed in auction listings.

- Performance standards are changing. Buyer feedback, DSRs, and other incidents that get resolved successfully (with your buyer) will no longer count against you. eBay says they're going to concentrate on what matters most.

- Return policies have been tweaked. Beginning in October of 2016, sellers will have the option to exchange or replace items, rather than to just give refunds.

- Turbo Lister is being phased out in June of 2017. Many of its features will be incorporated into the new seller hub.

- Finally, category updates are ongoing. As eBay continues its move to be more like Amazon, sellers need to update listings to add category specific information.

Overall, the changes reflect a more focused eBay. They are looking at the new online marketplace and making changes to ensure the site stays relevant to shoppers. That's good news for everyone. Buyers find more items they want, need and are willing to spend their money on, and sellers will hear the jingle where it counts—in their pocketbook.

- eBay decided mobile is where sales are moving. They announced the end of active content in listings beginning in June of 2017 to provide mobile users a better experience. eBay also created a new view item feature for mobile. It displays a 250-character text-only description to mobile users. The idea is to provide relevant details—quickly, for time conscious mobile shoppers.

- In a move to be more like Amazon, eBay is expanding product reviews to more categories and products. Their research shows product reviews keep buyers on the site longer and increase sales as much as 18 percent.

Again, the updates come from a milder, but still money-grubbing eBay. While Amazon, and other online retailers, make their money on the backend, eBay continues to take their cut on both ends of the transaction.

That's not a problem—if they can draw more active buyers to the site. Until they do that, eBay needs to get its house in order.

Table of Contents

Introduction 1

Why listen to me? 5

What's in a Title? 8

Illustrations 12

Item Description 21

Price your items to sell 33

Seller Reputation or feedback 38

Top 10 Tools to Help You Sell On eBay 45

Top 10 Tips to grow your eBay Business 49

Top 5 Reasons Why You Need to Sell Off eBay 62

Seller Profiles 64

    My eBay Story 66

    John – Sports Cards 74

    Jim – Part Time eBayer 80

    Sarah – eBay Educational Specialist 83

    Barb – eBay Newbie 87

    Davis – High School Student 90

    Terry – Automobile Internet Manager 93

Read These Books Next..97
Bonus Excerpt..100

Introduction

In an ideal world, there wouldn't be any need for a book like this. Every item you list on eBay would attract hundreds of bidders That 2017 Lincoln penny you got in change this morning, and listed on eBay as soon as you got home, would be feeling the love, and drawing hundreds of dollars in bids.

Unfortunately, the sad fact is less than forty percent of the auctions posted on eBay sell. Put in words just about anyone can understand—**three out of five items you try to sell – Won't Sell - Period**.

Sorry to be the one to break it to you. Most eBay books make it sound like a sure thing that you're going to sell every item you list for sale on eBay.

Contrary to popular belief – "List it and they will buy it" is not a viable eBay strategy. Just because you decide to sell an item doesn't mean people will magically flock to it, or bid on it.

Selling on eBay is all about getting your listings noticed. No matter how unique or extraordinary the item you're selling is, no one can buy it if they can't find it.

eBay marketing can be summed up in five simple words: title, illustration, description, price, and reputation.

This book is going to help you fine tune each of these eBay marketing strategies, so you can up your odds, and have a better chance of making a sale each time you come up to bat.

1. **Title**. Hands down, your title is the number one marketing tool available to you on eBay. eBay gives you eighty characters to describe your item. Make use of every one of them to ensure your item is visible to the largest number of viewers possible.

2. **Illustration**. You've heard the old saying "a picture is worth a thousand words." On eBay, that

saying goes double. The more high-quality pictures you post with your listing, the better the chances are you will sell your item, and get more money from it.

3. **Description**. A good description complements your title and illustrations. This is where you get the opportunity to drive home how great your item is, what condition it is in, and how great it would be to own one of these. Five or ten words will not cut it here. Tell a great story. Connect the dots, so that people understand why they need to buy your item.

4. **Price**. Your title, illustration, and description are all wasted if you place the wrong price on your item. Price your item too high, and no one will want it, price your item too low, and you leave profit on the table. Pricing is part science and part art. We will explore price in much more detail later in this guide.

5. **Reputation**. If you don't have good feedback, no one will buy from you. *On eBay, all you've got is your name.* Face the fact: **You're going to live and die by your feedback.** No matter how unfair

it sounds, do whatever it takes to make your customers happy.

That's all it takes. Follow these five simple steps. You will have a better chance to sell every item you list on eBay

We're also going to look at selling beyond eBay. For many sellers, this can mean pushing your sales out to Amazon, eBid, eCRATER, Etsy, and bidStart. Other sellers may decide to go it alone and start a website. Whichever you choose, we will give you some ideas to make the transition easier.

Why listen to me?

Hey there, Nick Vulich here.

If you're like me, I'm sure you're probably a little skeptical about taking advice from someone without knowing a little bit about them first.

I've been selling on eBay since 1999. Most of my online customers know me as history-bytes. I've also operated as *It's Old News*, Back Door Video, and Sports Card One.

I've sold 30,004 items for a total of $411,755.44 over the past fifteen years. That's just on my history-bytes id. I've taken a break from selling on eBay and Amazon to concentrate on writing and coaching, but I keep my hat in the game—constantly keeping in touch with sellers, and reading the latest reports on e-commerce.

I've been an eBay Power Seller, or Top-Rated Seller, for most of the past fifteen years, which means I've paid my dues and met eBay's tough sales and customer satisfaction goals.

    E-commerce 2017 is the thirteenth book I have written about how to sell on eBay. The first two, *Freaking Idiots Guide to Selling on eBay*, and *eBay Unleashed* are aimed more towards beginners. *eBay Subject Matter Expert* suggests a different approach to selling on eBay – building a platform where customers recognize you as an expert in your niche and buy from you because of your knowledge in that field. *Sell It Online* gives a brief overview of selling on eBay, Amazon, Etsy, and Fiver. *How to Make Money Selling Old Books & Magazines on eBay* talks specifically about what I know best, how to sell books and periodicals on eBay. *eBay Bookkeeping Made Easy* helps sellers understand how to keep track of the money they are earning, and how to take advantage of the tax code to make even more money. *eBay Shipping Simplified* helps sellers determine the best way to ship their items, and how to use eBay's shipping tools to make the task easier. It also has a primer on international shipping and how to use third party shipping providers such as Stamps.com and Endicia.

    eBay 2015 (also known as *eBay Money Machine*) is my longest book to date and encapsulates everything sellers need to know to start and grow their eBay business. *eBay*

2016 takes a different approach—showing sellers how to increase sales by employing a well thought out social media marketing campaign using Facebook, Twitter, Pinterest, and other sites. It also takes a close look at blogging for online sellers, and how to fund special projects using Kickstarter.

This book is a serious rewrite of my book *eBay 2014*. Pretty much everything has been rewritten and revised with up-to-date information. It should help to help tie up all the loose ends so that you can sell successfully on any e-commerce platform.

Let's get started.

What's in a Title?

eBay gives you eighty characters to describe your item. Your goal is to cram every detail and keyword you can into those eighty characters.

Your title is how people find the items you sell. eBay uses the words in your title to determine who sees the stuff you sell. Because of this, it's important to have every possible word or combination of words someone might search by in the title.

Your title doesn't have to read well or even make sense to be effective. It just needs to contain as many keywords as possible to maximize the chances it will be displayed when someone searches for a similar item.

Unfortunately, many people waste this valuable real estate trying to get cutesy or to write a sentence that makes sense. The fact is no one is going to search for, "very nice," "awesome," "great," or "one-of-a-kind." You would be much better off giving a professional descriptor like "near-mint" or "MS65," because these are terms collectors use.

Here are some tips to help you write more effective titles.

1. **Include as many keywords as possible**. You've got eighty characters. Use as many of them as you can in each title you write. Don't worry that your title doesn't make sense. Include all the keywords you think someone would use to describe the item you are selling.

2. **Double Check Your Spelling**. To get discovered by the maximum number of people, use proper spelling. If you're in doubt, use spell-check.

3. **Avoid using adjectives and descriptive phrases**. Save all the adjectives and descriptive phrases for your item description. No one searches for "very nice" – "LQQK" – or "WoW!"

4. **Avoid excess capitalization**. No one likes being shouted at, or knowing someone is working too hard to sell them. If you absolutely must use all

capitalization, only do it to one word, not your entire title.

5. **Use the correct terms.** If you are unfamiliar with the item you're selling, take a moment to Google it. One thing I've discovered over the years is people love to email you and criticize you when you misspell a word, put an item in the wrong category, or describe it wrong. Sometimes it feels like they're crawling out of the woodwork and gunning for you.

6. **Include common misspellings.** If the item you sell is frequently misspelled, include the misspellings in your title if you have room.

7. **Don't use abbreviations.** Abbreviations confuse your customers. If there is any doubt, spell it out. If you don't have room in your title for the word you want to use, chose another word with a similar meaning. The exception here would be commonly accepted abbreviations on eBay. NWT – New with tags, NIB – New in box, BNWT – Brand new with tags, FS – Factory sealed.

With all of that said, one of the hardest things for many sellers to do is decide which keywords to put in your title.

Perhaps, the easiest way to determine which keywords to include in your title is to look at other auctions for similar items. How do they describe the item? What keywords do they use? What words do you see show up in all the auctions?

After you've made the above list, take a minute to put yourself in the buyer's shoes. What words would you use to describe the item you're selling? Those are the keywords you want to include in your title.

Illustrations

Pictures sell stuff.

(eBay's new rules require you to upload at least one photo with every item, even if you use their catalog. All images need to be at least 500 pixels along the longest end; 1600 pixels are suggested to take maximum advantage of their image enhancements.

Another change in the image policy concerns watermarks, and text in pictures. You cannot watermark your image with your business name or logo. They also no longer let you include text in your gallery image.)

Make no mistake about it, very few people are going to buy your item if you don't include at least one picture. More pictures are always better.

Ask yourself this, would you shell out $400 for a used laptop if you couldn't see a picture of it first?

Now, what if I was selling a rare Hummel figurine and my description said it was in mint condition except for a small chip at the bottom of one leg, but I just showed one picture of the entire figurine. You'd probably have some lingering doubts about that chip, wouldn't you? As a seller, I could have easily moved you past those reservations by including several close-up pictures of the chipped area. That way you could decide for yourself, whether the chip is a bid stopper or not.

Take a good look at every item you sell. Put yourself in the buyer's shoes. What parts of the item would you need to see to decide if you want to buy that item? For a baseball card, you obviously need to see the front and back of the card. If you're selling a laptop, you probably want a picture of it with the Windows logo on the screen for proof it works. You would also want to have a photo to show any accessories offered with the laptop—cords, cases, manuals, discs, and anything else included in the auction.

If you sell clothes, check out how the bigger sellers do it. Many of them have male and female manikins to model their clothes on. This gives potential buyers a better reference for what they are buying, rather than just looking at a flat picture of a blouse or pair of jeans. Another thing the top sellers do is to include close-up pictures of designs, and any flaws they have described.

Here's the advice I gave about using pictures in my other book, *Freaking Idiot's Guide to Selling on eBay*. It's still solid advice on how to include photos in your item descriptions.

> *You can have the best title, a great description, and a killer price, but if your pictures suck you're not likely to make a deal.*
>
> *When people are ready to buy something, especially expensive items, they demand great pictures. The best example you can find here is your local car dealer. They don't stop with one picture. Most often you will find twenty to twenty-five pictures for every car they are selling. Your car dealer knows most customers shop on the internet before they come in.*
>
> *As a result, dealers give you a virtual tour of the car with the pictures they take. On the outside, they show you front, back, and both sides. There is at least one picture of*

the engine, a view into the trunk, the upper dashboard, the odometer showing the mileage, the floor – front and back, and close-ups of any damage.

You can learn a lot about the type of pictures you need by studying car dealer listings. The lighting is always perfect. Every picture is perfectly centered. They never put in a bad picture. They know one bad picture can kill the whole deal.

Plan your pictures the same way. You want at least one overall view of your item. You want detailed close-up pictures of any designs. If there is damage – don't just say it in the description. Include one or two pictures of the afflicted area. Let potential buyers decide for themselves how bad the damage is.

eBay lets you upload 12 free pictures with every listing. Include as many as you need to tell your story.

Let's take a closer look at how you can make sure you always have the best pictures available for your eBay listings.

1) **Pay attention to where you take your pictures**. A lot of sellers photograph their items in a messy room where you can see all the clutter in the background of their picture. Right away that makes buyers question how well you cared for the item.

Don't do this...

Here's a recent picture posted in an eBay auction. The description was just as bad, "This auction is for a 1955 Topps #50 Jackie Robinson card. This card is in -VG condition."

Other people, post pictures of several other items they are selling as well. Often, booksellers show a whole run of thirty or forty volumes of books from the same series, even though the auction they are listing is for just one book. That confuses potential bidders because you're sending out mixed signals. A lot of people only read the title, and look at the pictures, before they bid. When they don't receive all the items you showed in the picture, you're setting yourself up to receive negative feedback.

I used to include a scan of the title page to the magazine my articles were from in each of my listings. In each listing, I told people the illustration was shown to verify the date of publication only; it did not come with the actual item I was selling. I did, however, give instructions on how they could right-click on the item and print a copy if they would like one. I still had unhappy customers, because they didn't take the time to read the fine print, so I soon stopped including these pictures in my listings. It made for a lot fewer problems.

2) **Use a light box**. I found one on eBay several years ago for about $50.00. It's basically a frame with a cloth draped on each side, sort of like a tent. You get several small floodlights that provide you with proper lighting. My light box came with five different colored backdrops so I could vary the background if I chose to. Depending on the type and size of items you sell, you can find light boxes in a variety of sizes.

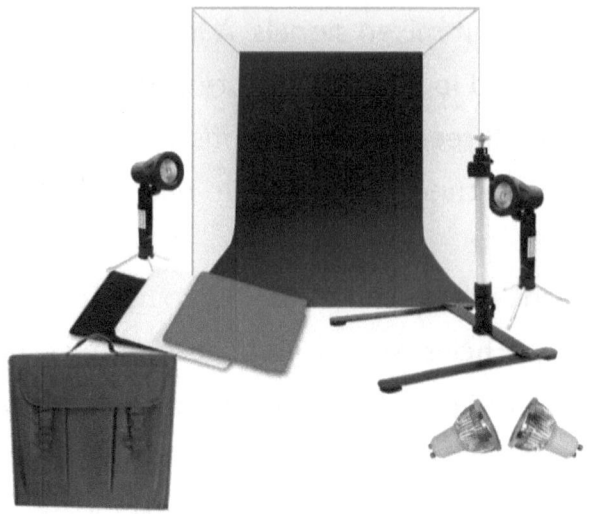

A light box lets you isolate your subject and surround it with nice even lighting. This prevents reflections that can keep people from getting a good clear look at your item. It also shows your item against a nice solid background, so it stands out.

3) **Use natural light if it is available**. Sunlight gives you better lighting for your pictures. Just be sure you aren't shooting pictures in the heat of the day, where the light may be too harsh.

4) **Shoot pictures from different angles**. Your item has many features. Capture it from as many different angles

as you can. This way, potential buyers can see all the details and features of what you are selling.

Put yourself in the customer's shoes and think about what they would want to see. If you sell an item that lights up don't just show a picture of it, include a picture with it fully lit up. If you are selling a leather billfold with a hand tooled design, show several close-up pictures of the design. A model car should be treated just like a real car. If the doors and hood open, take pictures of it. If it's a convertible, and the top comes off, include pictures with the top on and off.

5) **Use a tripod**. If your hand shakes, even a little, it can make for a fuzzy or blurry picture. Tripods help you take better pictures.

6) **Take close-up photos**, especially for smaller items like coins, stamps, or jewelry. Use the macro function on your camera. Shoot the picture as close-up as you can. Try to make it look like the buyer could just reach out and touch your item.

7) **Add a familiar item for contrast on size**. If you're selling a book, photograph it next to a ruler to give buyers a sense of what size your item is. Saying 10

inches is one thing. When you photograph your item next to the ruler it drives the concept home. You can do the same thing if you're selling, buttons, pins, or jewelry. Photograph the item next to a dime or a quarter. People will instantly make the size connection.

8) **Don't use flash**. When you use flash, it can cause your pictures to look distorted or blurry.

Item Description

Writing an eBay item description is a lot like crafting a short story. The more details and personality you put into it, the better the chances are it's going to engage potential buyers, and get them to bid on your item.

The journalist's toolkit includes the questions: Who, what, where, when, why, and how. Answer as many of these questions as you can in each item description. You will sell more items. Leave any of them out, and people are going to have unanswered questions about what you are selling.

Who. Buyers want to know who made the item you're selling. Is it an Apple, Nike, or JVC. If you're selling a book, tell people who the author is. Give as much information as you can about who made the item, what the brand is, or any other identifying names you find on it. If it's a name most people won't recognize, add a few lines to tell them who made it, and why that's important.

What. Tell people exactly what you are selling. While it may be obvious to you, many people aren't going to understand, even if you include plenty of pictures. Your job is to tell people what your item is, and what it does.

Don't say you have an iPad. Tell them you have "an iPad Mini, and it's great when you're on the go. Just put it in your pocket, and you always have the internet and all of your contact info close by." If you're selling a book, tell people what the actual title is! I don't know how many books I've seen listed as an old book about "cowboys, Indians, and cavalry fighting Sitting Bull on the western plains." That's a great combination of keywords, but you still need to say what it is you are selling.

Where. Tell people where your item was made. Is it a Carson City silver dollar, or was it coined at the Philadelphia Mint? Is it an original Black Forest cuckoo clock, or is it a reproduction clock made in Taiwan? Don't leave people guessing, tell them what they need to know.

People also want to know where the item is located. If there are a lot of similar items available on eBay, often people will choose to purchase items located closer to them so that they can save money on shipping.

When. When was your item made? Is it the most recent model of iPhone, or is it a first-generation model. If you sell collectibles, people want to know when it was made. If you are unsure, mention what era it is from.

Here are a few examples:
1. 1950's era Baseball cards
2. Turn of the century sports card memorabilia
3. 1955 Topps Hank Aaron baseball card in near mint condition

Why. Tell people why they need it. "This 1955 Hank Aaron Topps card is one of the keys to completing this vintage set. This one is in near mint condition and can easily be one of the highlights of your collection."

"Golden era comic books are getting harder to find, especially without torn pages or small rips in the spine. Snap this one up now, while you still can."

Give them a compelling reason why they need to buy your item – NOW!

How. Tell potential buyers how the piece was made. Was it hand-crafted? Was it made by a colony of elves in the Middle Earth? Or was it made at the Tootsie Roll factory on Cicero Avenue in Chicago?

Tell buyers how you are going to ship their item. Are you shipping by USPS, UPS, or FedEx? If you sell delicate collectibles like a vintage doll, Hummel figurine, or china set, tell people how carefully you package their items, so there won't be any damage during shipping.

Some things are better suited to telling a story than others. Look at the description I wrote for an 1836 copy of the Annals of Congress. I paid $8.00 for it on eBay and resold it four weeks later for $327.00. The guy I bought it from listed a group of old Government books in fair to average condition. As a result, I bought eight volumes for $63.00 and sold them for just over $2000.

A lot of times, how much money you make, and how many bidders you get, is determined by how good of a story you can tell.

Here is my description of that book.

> *This is an awesome book! It's old and does have a few problem areas I want to*

share with you. It was published in 1836. It has a brown leather cover, and as you probably know, leather starts chipping and flaking when it gets to be this age, so you need to be careful, or you will have brown leather all over your hands and clothes. The front cover is detached. I still have it, and it is in excellent shape. You can check out the picture, and see for yourself. The spine has some chipping, but it is intact. And the nice thing is, there is a ribbed area containing the title and date range, and that is all still there too.

And, did I mention, this book is stamped right inside on the first few pages, "Congressional Library." That means this book was in Washington when Abraham Lincoln and Daniel Webster were there. Did they page through it? I can't promise you anything, but it's possible.

This book contains some fantastic information. It seems there was some trouble brewing down in Texas around this time. Some of the page headers mention – Texas Independence, Conflict in Texas,

> Movement of Santa Anna's Army, and the Alamo. And, then there are other mentions about canals, roads, Post Office Department, and military fortifications.
>
> This volume is part three of a longer series of books from the Congressional session that year. I'm not sure how many volumes there were altogether.
>
> It's a one of a kind collectible. Feel free to contact me with any questions.

Other times you may just want to play with people's heads, and see if you can make a listing go viral. Consider this one.

> Aunt Edna died in the upstairs bedroom over a hundred years ago, but over the years many people in the family have thought she still might be there. Grandma remembers seeing her on the stairs one night when she was a kid. They were having a sleepover, and Edna appeared on the stairs out of nowhere, and then she was gone. Mom and her sisters remember dresser drawers being

slammed open and shut with nobody around to do it when they were kids.

Me, I don't remember anything. I was out of town last week, but when I came home, dad was going on and on about all the noise one night in the hall by the little bathroom. No one was upstairs at the time, and it was scaring the bejeezus out of mom, she's 86 now.

He'd read that if you put peanut butter in a Mason jar, sometimes that was a good way to lure ghosts. That night he set out a couple of jars with just a dab of peanut butter, and then he waited. The way he tells it, it was just after midnight, he heard the clinking of glass, and he jumped out and slapped the cover on that Mason jar – right quick like.

Caught her, he did, and that's how Aunt Edna came to be in this Mason jar, her ghost that is.

Anyway, we were figuring she's been in our family long enough. This is a great chance for someone else to have her, Mason jar and all. Just be careful not to open the *cap. She's probably not going to fall for that same trick twice.*

Don't be afraid to have fun with your item description. You're selling your stuff to real people. Many of them will enjoy a little humor, as long as you don't forget to include all of the details they need to make an informed decision.

That brings us to my next point. **Full disclosure is not an option**. If you want to continue selling on eBay, you need to tell people, the good, the bad, and the ugly, about every item you sell.

Imagine how disappointed you'd be if you ordered a gently used pair of Guess jeans online, and when you receive them you discover the stitching is coming undone in some of the seams, and there are faint grass stains on one of the knees. You'd be pissed off because the seller didn't mention either of those defects in their listing. Maybe they showed pictures, but they weren't clear enough or focused well enough to call out these issues.

When you write an item description, it needs to tell all the great things about the item you are selling, but it also needs to slow things down for a minute and say hey

– this item is great, but you should also know it has a few problems.

A funny thing happens when you tell people the item you're selling has some problems:

1. Buyers say, "Hey, I can trust this guy." He's not just trying to bullshit me about how good this thing is because he's also sharing what's wrong with it.

2. They tell themselves—maybe the problems mentioned aren't so bad, and maybe they can live with them.

3. People are more likely to bid on your item because they feel you're honest with them. This can make your so-so thing more desirable than another guy's mint item, because his description doesn't talk about flaws, and with any used item, there's bound to be something wrong with it. Tell people what's wrong with your stuff, and you will diffuse a lot of their concerns about buying from you.

Put a more positive spin on many of the defects your items have.

Here's an excellent description for a vintage baseball card:

> This vintage 1955 Topps Jackie Robinson card has been the highlight of my collection for years. I'm not a sports card expert so keep in mind the things I'm going to tell you are just my opinion. The colors are bright and clear. The top right corner has a small ding to it, nothing major, but you may want to keep that in mind when making your decision on this one. And, as you can tell from the second picture I've included the centering on the reverse side is just a little off. With all of that said it's been a great card for me, and one of the first cards I've shown anyone who has taken the time to look at my baseball card collection.
>
> The wife wants to take a vacation this year, so it's got to go. My loss is sure to be your gain. Place your bid today.

Compare that to the standard description.

> *1955 Topps Jackie Robinson Card. Very Good to Fine condition, with a small bang to upper right corner.*

Which one would you bid on? Which one do you think is going to attract more bids and higher offers? The first one of course. It's the same card, but the way the seller described it makes it sound unique, and more like something you've just got to have.

One more example and we will end our discussion of descriptions.

> *I came across this book several years ago, and everyone I show it to thinks it's one of the coolest things they've ever seen. It's called* **The Emigrant's Guide** *to Iowa and was published in Davenport, Iowa in 1855. It's a small book, 5" across and about 7" tall, and has 233 pages. Now the condition is not the greatest. The cover is red, and if you check out some of my pictures, you can see the spine is in pretty rough shape. There's a big chunk missing at the top. Other than that, it's all held together well, with no loose*

pages or anything. Inside there is some minor age spotting, but all the pictures and illustrations are in great shape. I counted seven pictures as I was flipping through this book, one of them is of the Old Capitol in Iowa City, and another is of cows grazing in some western Iowa pastures. If you're interested in Iowa history or are just looking for some unique piece of Iowa's past, this book could be the right choice for you.

It's got all the details you need to know. It tells a great story about the item to draw you into it. Give this method a shot with some of your listings. See what happens.

Price your items to sell

Pricing is one of the trickiest parts of selling on eBay or any online site for that matter.

Price your item too high, and no one will buy it. Price your item too low, and you will leave profit on the table. The problem is there is no one hundred percent perfect method for pricing your item right out of the box. Pricing is more of a process, especially if you are selling multiple copies of an item.

For some items, pricing is straightforward. Commodity items people buy every day like foodstuffs, DVD's, books, electronics, all sell in a very close price range. If you step out of the accepted price range for the item, your sales will dry up quicker than you think.

Perhaps, the easiest way to price your item is to search eBay to see how much similar items have sold for. To do this, use the Advanced Search function.

To access the Advanced Search function, go to the top of the eBay page. To the right of the search box, you will see the word **Advanced** just after the big blue Search box. Go ahead and click on the word **Advanced**.

Type in the name or description of the item you want to search for. Scroll down a little further where it says search including and check the box by **Completed Listings**. Then click enter. This returns a list of all the ended listing for that item within the past thirty days. Items listed in green are items that have sold.

Once you've done this, you can see a list of completed items on eBay. The non-sold listings appear for thirty days; sold listings appear for ninety days. After it returns this list, you have the option to narrow your search down even further by clicking on active listings (with bids) or completed listings.

The great thing here is you can see how much items similar to yours have recently sold for.

By looking through completed listings, you can easily find the price range your item has sold in. No more guessing about how to price your items.

The way I use the information is to look through the titles to find items most similar to mine. Each time I click on an item I take a few notes about any keywords the seller used in the title and item description. I also make a note of the selling price. If it was an auction item, I mark down the starting price. Next, I look at shipping to determine if the seller offered free shipping or the options and prices they offered for shipping. Another thing you want to note is the category the item was listed in.

After you do this four or five items, you will have plenty of information about how to write your item description and title. You should also get an excellent idea of how much you can get for your item.

At this point, we're almost ready to start pricing your item. Before you stop doing your research, I'd suggest you click into two or three of the items that sold for the highest prices. Look over your notes. Did these listings say anything different than the other ones? Specifically, did they offer a more detailed description? Did they use different keywords in the title? Did they start at a lower price? Did they use a buy-it-now?

Now, you need to decide on a pricing strategy.

Some people swear by starting everything at 99 cents or $9.99 and letting the market determine the price. The problem with this approach is it only works for certain categories of items. If you sell stuff that always closes in a tight price range like electronics, cell phones, iPhones, iPads, and the like, starting your item at 99 cents is going to bring in the maximum number of bidders, and will generally bring you the highest price possible for each item.

If you sell one of a kind items collectibles, and other low demand items, starting your item at 99 cents is going to be a disaster. What's going to happen in nine out of ten cases is, if your item sells at all, it's going to sell for 99 cents, or $1.04.

A better pricing strategy with many items is to price them at the lowest price you are willing to accept. Then add a buy-it-now at what you would like to get. If you are selling your item in a fixed price format, set the price somewhat higher than you hope to get, and add best offer to it.

What if you're selling something unique, that isn't currently available on eBay? How do you price your item then?

If it's something you have a lot of or a lot of similar items the best thing you can do is experiment with different prices. Determine which one sells the most items.

Let me give you an example. I sell old magazine articles, removed from bound publications. All I'm selling is a few sheets of old paper. I have a few competitors on eBay, but not many.

When I first started to sell magazine articles, I priced them at $12.99, and they sold well. After six months, I increased my price to $15.99, and then $19.99, and then $25.99, and sales kept growing each time. When I stretched it to $27.99, sales started to slow down. As a result, I knew my optimal price range was somewhere between $19.99 and $25.99.

I found my sweet spot in auction pricing the same way. I started my items at $9.99, and many of them sold. Then I added Buy-it-Now at 15.99, $19.99, and $25.99. Once again $25.99 provided the most conversions, so that's the formula I went with – a $9.99 starting price, with a $25.99 Buy-it-Now.

It was a great price strategy. It worked for years.

The next thing you know, eBay decided they wanted to be more like Amazon, and to become more of a marketplace so they could lure in the big sellers like Best Buy and Toy-R-Us.

One of the things they did was to change the emphasis to fixed price listings rather than auctions. That sent me back to the drawing board, and once again, I reinvented my eBay business, this time focusing it on fixed price listings, with a just a scattering of auction listings.

Seller Reputation or feedback

The only thing an eBay seller has is his good name or his reputation.

Feedback on eBay gets earned each time you complete a successful transaction. If buyers are happy, they can leave feedback. Feedback is based on a five-star rating system, plus a one-line comment where the seller can say something good or bad about your product or service.

In an ideal world, anything above four would be passing, but in eBay's convoluted grading system anything less than a 4.8 average is marginal, and if you fall below a 4.6 average feedback score, you are in danger of losing your buying and selling privileges.

You can check your feedback score at any time by visiting your seller dashboard.

Seller performance numbers		Updated daily
3 months (12/01/12 - 02/28/13)		Transactions: 192 See your reports
Average detailed seller ratings	Your average	Low ratings (1s and 2s)
Item as described	4.96	0.52% (1)
Communication	5.00	0.00% (0)
Shipping time	5.00	0.00% (0)
Shipping and handling charges	4.96	0.00% (0)
Buyer Protection cases		Your percentage (count)
Opened cases		0.00% (0)
Closed cases without seller resolution		0.00% (0)

Performance numbers are from transactions with buyers in the United States.

Using the radio bar, you can view your rating for the previous three months, or for the last twelve months. It gives you your DSR ranking in each category, your percentage of low ratings where you received one or two stars, the number of transactions you completed in the period, and your percentage numbers for buyer protection cases filed.

One area all sellers are susceptible to problems in is shipping and handling fees. Even if you charge reasonable shipping fees, or subsidize part of the shipping costs, you are always open to customer perceptions. Some clients think five dollars is unfair for shipping a fifty-pound computer printer; other buyers will be ok with a five-dollar charge for sending a few pieces of paper. The thing is you never know which type of customer you're going to get.

One way to avoid a negative item strike for shipping fees is to offer free shipping. If you offer free shipping, eBay automatically gives you a Five-Star rating for the shipping and handling category. So, if this is an area that's always dragging your DSR rating down, you may want to find a way to offer your customers free shipping.

Shipping and handling time is a category you have limited control over.

All you can do is mail items immediately or within your promised time frame. Then, upload tracking information into the system as soon as possible. If you do this every time, you can prove you did everything possible to get the item on its way quickly.

The sad thing is you can still run into snags.

Sometimes the mailman cannot deliver the item, so he will leave a tag for the customer telling them they need to pick up their package at the post office. The problem is the tag can blow away, or someone else may get the tag, and not show it to your customer. Other times, the mailman may mess up and deliver your item to the wrong house. It happens every day. If you provide tracking on all your items, you can usually figure out what happened, and tell customers exactly where the hold-up is.

Another problem area is international shipping. Nine times out of ten everything goes as it should, and your customer will receive their package within seven to ten business days, sometimes much faster. Other times, the item can get caught up in customs, or held up at a post office somewhere along the way, and take six to eight weeks or more to deliver.

The best you can do here is to set realistic expectations. A good way to do this is to let international buyers know up front in your auction description what they can expect regarding delivery times. I like to say something like this, "All international shipping is by first class mail. Standard delivery time is two to three weeks, but can take as many as six weeks depending on customs and handling times." This way, when an international customer writes you a few days, or weeks later wondering when they can expect delivery, you can refer them back to your original information. Most customers understand when I use this approach because the information is not coming at them out of the blue like I am making excuses. Instead, it is just a matter of reinforcing what you already told the customer.

Item as described and communication are all about you.

If you followed the information presented earlier in this guide and provided an accurate and honest item description, supplemented with several great pictures you should eliminate ninety-nine percent of items not as described cases.

Take my sales as an example. I sell magazine articles and pictures extracted from old magazines. This can cause confusion with some customers because even though I tell them it is a "magazine article carefully removed from a vintage magazine," I still get emails or feedback saying, "I was expecting a book, and all I got was a page taken out of a book or magazine." The truth is I tell people three times in each item listing what they are buying. "It is not a book or a complete journal, just an article."

So, when I get a bad feedback or a message from a customer demanding a refund, I tend to get a little-pissed off, but I bite my tongue and send them the following response.

"I'm sorry you're not happy with the item you purchased. I can understand your frustration I would feel the same way. Here at history-bytes, we do our best to describe every item we sell. Each item is carefully labeled with the item description as 'a vintage magazine article carefully extracted from an old magazine, not the entire magazine.' If you are unhappy with your item I will be more than happy to take it back and offer you a full refund, shipping included. Keep me advised."

When you do this, it throws the ball back into the customer's court. I politely tell them what they should already know if they had taken the time to read the auction description. At the same time, if they are unhappy, they know I will take the item back for a full refund. In most cases, the customer writes back and tells me that even though the item isn't quite what they expected, they are happy with it, and will keep it.

Out of thirty thousand sales over the past fourteen years, I've had fewer than ten items returned, so I can guarantee you this method will work for you.

You're also going to receive frivolous complaints from customers trying to shame you into giving them a discount. I've probably had at least a hundred people email to tell me the item I sent them was incomplete and either some pages or pictures were missing. Again, I know the odds of that are unlikely because I packaged and mailed the item myself. I follow the same path with these customers that I do with other customer service issues. I apologize and offer a full refund.

Once again, because I don't take the offensive or get mad, most of the customers tell me it's okay. They want to keep the item anyway, even though it is incomplete. Odds are they were just shooting for a discount. Otherwise, they would have returned the item if it was incomplete.

That brings us back to communication. Ninety-five percent of your customers don't require any special communication. If you mail their item on time and promptly upload tracking information your client is going to give you the five-stars.

The other five percent of customers have questions before or after the sale. If you get back to them within twenty-four hours and provide them with a friendly response, you will be okay. It's when you blow them off and don't bother to respond to repeated requests for more information you're going to have trouble.

Top 10 Tools to Help You Sell On eBay

eBay information

- **eCommerce Bytes**. If you're an online seller, you need to read this to keep up with what's going on. Ecommerce Bytes blog will keep you informed about what's happening in the world of online sales. Sign up for their daily email updates, and take a few minutes every day to read a few articles. They're short and informative.

- **Channel Advisor Blog**. This one contains a lot of information and reports about how to sell on eBay, strategies you can use, and it is more detailed than e-commerce bytes.

- **The Online Seller.** This e-zine gives a lot of great info about how to sell on eBay and other e-commerce sites. Some recent stories include – Selling on eBay as an eBay Consignment Specialist, Online Auction Sites Other Than eBay, and Is Selling on Etsy Right for You? (a multi-part series). Most of the articles are short, easy to read, and will get you thinking of ways to help grow your eBay business.

Auction Selling Tools

- **Auctiva** is the largest auction hosting and image hosting service. Fees range up to $40 per month depending on the number of images hosted. The major disadvantage with Auctiva is they are eBay specific and do not integrate with Amazon like some of the other services do.

- **Vendio** allows sellers to list and sync items on eBay and Amazon. Fees range from $24.95 to $149.95 depending upon your monthly dollar volume of sales, and the number of items you have for sale.

- **Ink Frog** is an eBay-specific auction and picture hosting service.

- **Channel Advisor** is a multi-channel e-commerce platform that allows you to sell on eBay, Amazon, Buy.com, Sears, and Newegg. They also can help with Social Media, paid search advertising, and planning selling strategies.

Mailing services

- **Stamps.com** is run by the United States Post Office and can help sellers mail their products more efficiently. When they use Stamps.com, sellers can import buyer information from eBay, Amazon, Etsy, and other marketplaces and print shipping labels on their home computers. Stamps.com will also print International mailing labels and customs forms. There are two levels of service: a free version for eBay sellers and a basic version for $15.99.

- **Endicia** offers some mailing services similar to Stamps.com. Their monthly fees start at $9.99.

They also allow merchants to add a logo to their labels to help promote their brand.

Multi-Channel Selling

- **Export Your Store** is a service that helps sellers to move their eBay store to the Amazon Marketplace easily. They offer syncing services to keep your eBay and Amazon stores up to date. The cost is $299 for the initial import (they will work with you on pricing for smaller stores), and $99 per month to sync your items.

Top 10 Tips to grow your eBay Business

Build your brand. Don't just make sales take the time to build your brand. People don't just buy Apple computers, iPhones, and iPads, they swear by them. They tell their friends about them. People write glowing reviews about items they like. Some of them even hit the Facebook like button.

Make your business likable. Be the business; people want to tell their friends about. When I first started out, I included a handwritten thank-you note with every item I sold. As my business grew, this got harder to do. One thing I did was to print up blank Thank-you cards with Vista Print. Whenever I make a large sale, I write a personalized note on one of these and include it when I mail my stuff.

Sometimes, for no reason at all, I send a card out to my better buyers. When I do this, I don't try to sell them anything. I just say "it was great doing business with you. I hope you enjoy your items. Have a great day, Nick."

I also built a website, digitalhistoryproject.com that I share with people who purchase from me. From time to time I post articles and pictures on it that I think my customers would enjoy. It's entirely free. They don't have to buy anything. But when they go there, it has links to my eBay and Amazon stores, and to some of my Kindle Books.

The website gives people one more way to connect with me, without my having to try and sell to them.

Build your brand to keep your customers coming back to you.

Experiment with new products. No one can make money selling the same products forever. People change. Their needs change. You need to change along with your customers and stay one step ahead of them, so you can have the products they want there and waiting for them when they are ready.

Don't be afraid to try new items. What's the worst that can happen? They won't sell. If this happens, forget about it, and move on to your next product.

No one hits a home run every time they're up to bat. You don't need to either. Just keep looking for new products. You will find yourself coming up with more winners than losers.

If you have any doubt about this strategy, look at Mountain Dew or Frito Lay. Every month they bring out a new version of their product. Ninety-nine percent of them disappear, but the winners stick around and help them enjoy increased sales.

Do the same thing to help grow your business.

Automate everything you can. Life is easier when you put things on autopilot.

When I first started, I used to leave all my feedback myself. When my sales reached 500 items per month, feedback became a burden, so I automated it. Now I don't need to worry about feedback. As soon as a customer makes their payment with PayPal, the system leaves feedback for me.

The same goes with my eBay listings. I always use *good till canceled* for my fixed price listings. That way I never need to do anything. They are always running. My auctions style listings work the same way. I set them to automatically relist a certain number of times if they don't sell. This way I don't need to do anything until they either sell or stop relisting.

If you want more time to run your business, or if you want to have more free time to spend with your family, put as many tasks as you can on autopilot.

Price doesn't matter. Contrary to what you think, you don't have to have the lowest price. Don't be afraid to be the highest priced seller. Often, price is only one of many factors that influence customers to buy from you.

Like any eBay seller, I have competitors, but I've always tried to set myself apart from the competition. To do this I offer a wide variety of items, tell an intriguing story where needed, offer quick shipping, and responsive customer service.

My thought is that if I offer a product people enjoy why shouldn't I charge a premium price?

When you do this, people perceive a higher priced item is more valuable. It is true there are always two or three other sellers on eBay who sell the same items I do, some of them at half the price, but a lot of sellers choose to buy from me anyway.

Why? Part of it is I've got great feedback. I also have one of the largest selections of vintage magazine articles available on eBay and have had for the last fourteen years. Because of this many of the customers who bought from me when I first started selling online, are still with me today. And, even when the economy is slow, I can count on making sales to them.

Free shipping may not be the answer. Don't let eBay bully you into offering free shipping. If you're thinking about offering free shipping, test, and test some more. Make sure it makes sense for you and brings in more sales.

eBay has done a lot of studies that show customers like free shipping. They also know from customer feedback shipping charges are one of the largest trouble areas on the site. Even if seller's charge reasonable shipping or offer discounted shipping, a lot of buyers think what you charge them is unfair.

My suggestion is that you should make sure free shipping is going to work for you before you roll it across all your items.

I offered free shipping several times. It never worked for me. Sales don't magically increase just because you offer free shipping. You can try to roll all the shipping costs or a portion of them into your selling price, but a lot of times, that just decreases your sales. Buyers are smart. They understand what you're doing.

Consumers know someone needs to pay for shipping. If they don't feel you're out to make a buck on it, they're going to buy from you.

If you are worried customers are going to balk at your shipping costs, tell people why you charge more. Do you sell delicate items in need of special care and packing? Explain how carefully you pack each item to ensure it will arrive safely. Better yet, shoot a video showing how carefully you pack your items and include it in every auction.

It's an old sales trick. Answer objections before they come up, and you will sell more items every time.

Have fun with what you do. If you enjoy what you do, people are going to know. They will see it in the way you word your auction descriptions and the way you respond to your customer service emails. Too many people come off as assholes in their auction descriptions. They have all these policies and list all sorts of warnings. You know the ones I'm talking about, they say –

- Your bid is a legally binding contract
- If you don't like our terms, don't bid
- Returns will not be accepted

- All items are sold "as is." Read the item description carefully, and make sure this is what you want, before bidding

I wouldn't buy anything from a seller who puts things like this in their product descriptions, even if I want the item they are selling. Life is too short to deal with assholes.

Lighten up!

Sell for a cause. If you want to make your items more visible on eBay, try listing your items in a charity auction.

eBay Giving Works lets sellers donate from 10% to 100% of the selling price of the items they sell to one of the charities listed with them. There are thousands of charities to choose from. If you've never sold through eBay Giving Works before, they don't just partner with the large national organizations like the American Red Cross and The United Way. They represent thousands of smaller regional charities as well.

I live in Davenport, Iowa. When I search Giving Works by location to find charities in my city, twelve organizations are listed.

- Disability Assistance Dogs

- K-9 Kindness Rescue, Inc.
- Humane Society of Scott County
- Quad Cities Affiliate of Susan G Komen for the Cure
- United Way of the Quad Cities
- Habitat for Humanity
- Storytellers International
- Adventure Christian Community Church of the Quad Cities
- Gateway Redevelopment Group
- Genesis Health Services Foundation
- King's Harvest
- St. Ambrose University Children's Campus

If I stretch my search out to within ten miles of Davenport, there are over twenty-five local charities I can sell for.

eBay makes it easy to sell for a charity. Just check the box while you're listing your item for sale, and choose what percentage of the sale you would like to donate. eBay credits a portion of your fees back to you.

Whenever I use charity auctions, my page views skyrocket. Frequently, page views increase two hundred to three hundred percent, especially when I partner with a larger charity.

Try a charity auction next time you sell on eBay. You will sell more items, and you will feel good about yourself.

Don't waste time going to the Post Office. There are a lot of services out there to help you ship your items. Use them to save time and money on shipping.

You can easily print all your postage through eBay or PayPal. Just choose the *Print Shipping Label* option.

Two other options are Stamps.com and Endicia. Both services charge monthly fees, but they give you more shipping options.

I use Stamps.com and have for over ten years. There is a $15.99 monthly fee, but it keeps me from having to go inside the Post Office three or four times a week. That's worth the money to me. When I use Stamps.com, I can mail international items by first class. If I send the same item using PayPal or eBay, the only shipping options are Priority and Express mail. Those services are way too expensive an option for me to offer to my customers.

Another benefit of using Stamps.com is it allows you to ship all your items from different marketplaces through one dashboard. Stamps.com lets you add multiple eBay stores, your Amazon store, and your Etsy store, so you can mail everything from one location. It's a whole lot quicker to use, and if you need to provide tracking information, it's available in one place.

Whichever service you choose, it will save you time and money on shipping.

Know your Numbers. A lot of eBay sellers have no idea how much money they're making or not making. They assume because money keeps flowing into their PayPal account things are good.

To make a profit selling on eBay, you need to know your numbers. Everything you do on eBay has fees associated with it. If you aren't careful, they can get the better of you – Fast!

Here are just a few of the fees and expenses you need to watch –

- eBay store fees
- Final value fees
- Auction Extras (bold, highlight, picture packs, etc.)
- Shipping
- Packing supplies
- Insurance fees
- Image hosting
- Service providers like Auctiva, Vendio, and Ink Frog
- Actual costs of the item you are selling

- Refunds for lost and disputed items
- Bookkeeping (whether you use an accountant or an online service like Outright)
- Gasoline
- Wear and tear on your car whenever you go to the Post Office or out to source items or purchase mailing supplies
- Computers, scanners, digital cameras, scales
- Broadband internet access
- Your time

Everything you do on eBay costs money. To make a profit, you need to understand what it costs you to sell an item.

If you pay five dollars for the item, you are selling, and it sells for ten dollars, that leaves you with a fifty percent profit. Or does it?

eBay fees are going to set you back at least $1.05. PayPal is going to take another .50 to process your transaction. If you have an eBay store or use a service like Auctiva, you may easily have another $1.00 into your auction. That brings your cost up to $7.55. So now you're at a $2.45 profit. If you offered free shipping, that's another $2.50 to $6.00 depending on the item you are selling, and how you ship it. Now you're losing money!

At the end of the day, it's easy to lose money selling on eBay. **If you don't know your numbers, you can easily fool yourself into thinking you're making money.**

Know your numbers, and what it's going to take to make a profit.

One other cost most people don't figure in is the cost of your time. If you spend ten hours a week selling on eBay and only make $25.00, that's $2.50 per hour. Only you can decide how much your time is worth.

Make time for yourself. Selling on eBay can be a great business, but it can soon become a prison, sucking you into working endless hours.

Most eBay sellers work at home. As a result, it's often hard to separate your personal life and your business life.

There's always one more item you can list for sale. You will find yourself constantly checking for emails, and answering customer inquiries at all hours of the day and night. And, there are always sales. You're going to find yourself checking them way too many times, especially when sales are a little slow.

As Detective Adrian Monk would say, "It's a blessing and a curse."

Unless you want to hate selling on eBay, find a way to shut it off, and make time for yourself. Decide on a cut-off time, and stick to it. No eBay after 5:00 pm; or no eBay on weekends.

Make time for yourself.

Top 5 Reasons Why You Need to Sell Off eBay

1. **Reach more customers.** While it's true eBay does have more buyers than all the alternatives (except Amazon), the fact is you need to do whatever it takes to attract new customers.

2. **Many customers are fed up with eBay.** Over the years eBay has alienated a lot of buyers and sellers, with their constant changes, and site revisions. "Best Match" became "no thanks" as it often made it harder for customers to find the items they wanted. Other people didn't like being told they couldn't pay with a check, cash, or money order.

3. **Nothing lasts forever.** As good as eBay is, and as long as they've been the big kid on the block,

sooner or later, some new guy is going to come along and push them aside. Remember F.W. Woolworths, Circuit City, or look at what happened to Blockbuster and J. C. Penney. Make sure you have a Plan B, just in case.

4. **You never know until you give it a try**. It's easy to say eBay alternative sites don't work, but you will never know if they work for you or not unless you try.

5. **A dollar is a dollar, no matter where you make it**. If you try a new site and you only make one sale a month, that's still extra money in your pocket.

Seller Profiles

Over the years I've had the opportunity to work with and talk to hundreds of eBay sellers. Some of them were brand new to eBay. Others have been selling for ten years or more.

Every one of them has a unique story about how they got started selling on eBay, and what they expect to take away from it.

Many people I know embraced eBay because it gave them a real opportunity to start a business with little or no risk other than the time they invested.

A lot of parents have looked at eBay as a chance to stay home with their children and be with them as they grow up.

For others, eBay has supplemented a lifetime of low-wage jobs. It has given them hope after being laid off from a lifelong career in corporate America.

Others have used their eBay incomes as a stepping stone to other careers. Many have become consultants or experts in the product lines they started selling on eBay. Some have become instructors and helped other people start and operate successful online businesses.

For me, eBay gave me extra money to buy new cars and a bigger house when I was working. After a corporate layoff in 2004, selling on eBay gave me the opportunity to build a robust and stable business of my own. Over the last five years, eBay has become my stepping stone to a new career in writing and helping other people learn how to sell on eBay.

The following section profiles some eBay sellers I have known, and the businesses they are running on eBay. I look forward to adding you to the list of eBay successes.

Good luck and great selling!

My eBay Story

(This is the bio I included in my first book **Freaking Idiot's Guide to Selling on eBay, How anyone can make $100 or more everyday selling on eBay**. I thought it might be helpful for everyone to read it over and see how I got started. Maybe it will give you some ideas.)

My story is typical of many eBay sellers.

I got my first taste of online auctions in 1999. I had been following eBay and Yahoo Auctions for some time. One day, I took the plunge. I bought a couple of baseball cards.

And then, I bought some more and some more. It was like an addiction.

One thing led to another, and then I had this crazy idea maybe I could sell some baseball cards, too. I bought "lots" of 1954 and 1955 Topps baseball cards thinking I could piece together a set. Many of the cards were lower grade, with creases and bruised corners, but they were a start.

When I got a better card, it went in my set. The other cards ended up in a cast-off pile. As time went by, I found myself with quite a few of these castoffs. And, they became my first foray into auction selling.

My auctions weren't anything special. I scanned a picture of the card, front and back, added a little description, and posted it on eBay. I priced most of them between $1.00 and $5.00 based on how mangled they were.

But, the thing is—people bought them. Sometimes I even had bidding wars erupt, where they would jump from $1.00 to $10.00 and even $20.00 occasionally. How cool is that?

This went on for six months, and I was doing ok. I wasn't making any money because even though I was selling several hundred dollars worth of cards a month, I was buying just as much or more. But it felt good because people were sending me money. Every day I received cash and checks in the mail, and dutifully I would package those baseball cards up, stuff them in an envelope, and send them off to their new owners.

It was fun. And, to make it more interesting, back in those days, people sent you cash. Many times, ten and twenty dollar bills fell out of those envelopes.

One day I had one of those epiphany moments. I was perusing through the auction listings and discovered a guy selling an old magazine article (not a whole magazine, just one section taken from a magazine). It made me stop. And think. What kind of a nutcase would buy, or sell, a magazine article?

I read his description. I looked at his pictures. He was asking $10.00.

I needed to know a little more. I looked at the other items he was selling. He had about fifteen or twenty magazine articles for sale. Some of them had bids. A couple of them were over $20.00.

I checked his sold history. Over the past six months, he had sold nearly one hundred magazine articles. Not bad for a few pieces of paper torn out of a musty old book.

I went back to selling my baseball cards. But over the next few weeks, my thoughts kept wandering back to that guy selling magazine articles. I like history. I love books. It seemed like something I could do.

My first step into this new venture was to purchase a copy of Harper's Magazine from 1865. It had a good mix of articles. Some items were on the Civil War. Others were about historical places and events.

My investment was a whopping $15.00. And, like just about all the items I sell, I bought it on eBay.

When my issue of Harper's arrived, I paged through it. Before I took it apart, I made a list of the articles I wanted to sell, how I was going to describe them, and how much I was going to ask for them.

Anyway, to make a long story short, I sold most of those articles quickly. My $15.00 investment turned into $250.00. And, like my venture with baseball cards, I bought more and more, and still more books to break apart and sell.

Today, I have over 6,000 items listed on eBay and just over 10,000 on Amazon.

Over the past thirteen years, I completed nearly 30,000 sales as history-bytes on eBay alone. I'm just ending my first year of selling on Amazon, and have racked up close to 200 sales there. It's proving to be a tough nut to crack compared to eBay, but I will make it happen.

***

After being laid off in 2004, I jumped into eBay full time. I went from making $500 a month to $5000 a month.

Before doing this, I read everything I could find about how to sell on eBay. I had someone design a custom template and eBay store interface for me. I plugged my picture into every auction listing hoping to build trust into my listings. I offered a "100% Money Back Guarantee – No Questions Asked."

I went from having 500 listings in my eBay store to maintaining almost 10,000 items listed for sale at any given time. I was listing 400 items a week, and mailing out nearly 150 packages every week.

It was more work than having a job. I don't think there was a single week that I clocked under 70 hours. It was a seven-day work week.

The story is the same for almost every full-time eBay seller I have ever talked with. It's a 24 / seven job.

You get hooked on it.

***

Many of my best sales came about by accident. Others happened because of deliberate planning, and a whole lot of luck.

I took a lot of chances growing my business.

I stretched the barrier every chance I could on pricing. Many sellers in my category were selling the same items I sold for a whole lot less. I asked $25.00 or $30.00. They asked $5.00 or $10.00 for the same thing. I decided long ago to go for the gusto. My items have always sold better at a higher price.

I found myself trying a lot of new things.

One of my great successes was selling newspapers. I bought every bound volume I could of the *Niles Weekly Register.* It was one of the first real National newspapers in America. Over time I was able to assemble almost a complete run from 1811 to 1833.

From 1812 to 1815, they contained significant accounts of battles and leaders in the War of 1812. I read through every paper and listed them on eBay one by one. I included excerpts from battlefield accounts in all of my listings. Two of them on the burning of the White House sold for $100 each. Another paper from 1811, contained a printing of the Declaration of Independence, side-by-side with Jefferson's notes for it. That one raked in $250.

I even tried bundling with a few of them. Two of our presidents, Thomas Jefferson and John Adams, died on July 4, 1826. Four papers profiled their lives, deaths, and news of their funerals. These articles sparked some of the hottest bidding any of my auctions ever received. They sold for was over $500.

Another time, I bid on an 1840's copy of George Catlin's **Letters and Notes**. I lost the bid. The book sold for over $500. But another seller emailed me to say she had a copy she was willing to part with for $200. I jumped on it and sold the individual prints for over $3500. It was an excellent score and brought me lots of new customers.

I stumbled across eight bound volumes of the **Annals of Congress** from the 1830's for $10 each. They included news about the battle of the Alamo and Mexican troop movements in Texas. The Mormon exodus from Illinois and Missouri was discussed over and over again, along with many other popular topics of the day. Once again, I sold individual pages about the Alamo and the Mormon's for $100 or more – each.

****

If I could tell sellers anything about eBay, it would be to develop a specialty that no one else is serving, and work it for all its worth.

Many of my customers have been with me since the beginning. They know I'm out there searching for new and unique things. They appreciate that and keep coming back to see what's next.

Over the years, I've sold items to the White House Historical Society, the Royal Museum in Jamaica, castles and historical societies all over the United States, Europe, Japan, China, Russia, Australia, and more. Hundreds of authors and publishers count on me for information when they are writing books and illustrating magazine articles and books.

Museums buy illustrations and articles every day to augment their displays.

Probably, the most off the wall sale I ever made was an article I found in a 1950's movie star magazine. There was a letter a from a pregnant movie star to her unborn daughter. Fifty years later, her daughter saw that article in one of my listings and purchased a letter from her mom that she had never seen, or even knew existed.

***

In the thirteen years that I've been selling on eBay technology has changed. People's wants and needs have changed. I now have a website, digitalhistoryproject.com. I'm offering many of my more popular magazine articles as Kindle and Nook Books.

Who knows where your eBay journey will take you?

John – Sports Cards

John began collecting sports cards as a kid. He got his start selling them in the early 1990's when he was still in college. After school, the sportscard market softened, and the show circuit fell apart, so John socked his cards away. Once or twice a year he would do a few shows, just to keep his hat in the game. Most times, he was lucky if he sold enough cards to pay his table fees.

In 2001 a friend introduced John to Yahoo auctions, and he caught the selling bug all over again. In the beginning, he would list ten or twenty cards per week and regularly sell twelve or thirteen of them.

One thing he noticed was online buyers weren't as worried about condition, as people at shows. In fact, many of his Yahoo customers were voracious consumers of filler cards (cards in fair to poor condition).

To keep up with the demand, he started buying "lots" of cards, or near complete sets and breaking them up. Often, he could sell the individual cards for $3.00 to $5.00 each. If he was lucky, there were a few cards in better condition that he could sell for $10.00 or $20.00.

Up to this point, he was selling cards from his collection and supplementing them with cards he bought online.

In 2002, he moved his business to eBay. The buyers were more reliable and paid for the items they bid on. Yahoo was littered with a lot of deadbeat buyers, and often, it was a crapshoot, waiting to see if they would pay or not.

The move to eBay exposed John to a larger audience. He began to sell more cards than ever before. One of the challenges now was getting enough cards to keep his sales growing. To meet the demand, he started going to bigger card shows and setting up tables just to buy cards, not to sell. He spent more time scouring eBay listings to grab any "lot" he thought gave him the potential to break up and sell the cards individually.

The strategy worked great. According to John, he "was working seventy even eighty hours a week just to keep up" with the demand. His fiancé even jumped in and helped with shipping. Many times, they mailed fifty to sixty packages per day.

In early 2008, John started selling high-end sports memorabilia – autographs, jerseys, and gloves. By the middle of the year business was taking off, and John borrowed more and more money to source better material.

September of that year things started to take a wrong turn. The government announced we were in a recession. By mid-October, sales were down twenty-five percent. John was starting to feel the hurt.

By January his sales were down fifty-one percent, and he was having trouble meeting his loan payments. John's first response was to cut prices. Many times, he was barely making a profit, or even losing money after covering his eBay fees.

2009 was a roller coaster ride of declining sales, price cutting, and fending off bankers as John tried to restructure his eBay business.

No matter what he tried, nothing seemed to work. Customers didn't respond to drastically lower prices, and when he tried to package lots to sell excess inventory to other dealers, none of them showed any interest either. Many other sports memorabilia dealers felt the hurt, too.

John saw a lot of his competitors disappear from eBay and was pretty sure he would suffer the same fate.

Finally, out of desperation, John partnered with an eBay consultant who helped him rebrand his business. One of the first things they did was to design a new logo and build a new eBay store with a fancier listing template.

John had an anchor store but didn't use any of its features. His designer changed that.

They used the custom pages to build John's brand, and tell people more about the items he sold. The consultant designed individual pages for sports cards, autographs, jerseys, bats, and gloves. The custom pages featured large pictures of items from each category and talked about how to put each type of collection together, how to take care of your things, and what to look out for when shopping so that you didn't get burned by fakes.

The consultants also showed John how to optimize his gallery pictures to help draw potential bidders into his auctions. Every picture was a close-up and taken with proper lighting. They added more pictures to each listing and made sure buyers could see a potential purchase from every angle.

John's storefront got a more colorful design. The landing page had category pages customers could click on to enter the individual listings.

Everything looked professional.

John changed his inventory and got rid of the less expensive items because they no longer fit in with the image he wanted to project. To do this, he sold the other stuff on a second eBay account.

The first month he made the change, John said he "had nightmares waiting to see what would happen." Sales picked up, slowly at first. He got more sales at higher prices than he'd seen in years.

Over the next six months, sales continued to grow. John noticed a lot of new customers along with many of the old ones starting to buy again.

John moved some of his business off eBay so that he wouldn't get caught off guard like he was last time. This time he opened a Yahoo store and got his designer to match its theme with his eBay store. The Yahoo store is making sales, but getting traffic to it is always a struggle.

John tried Google AdWords and added special inserts in each of his mailings. He has high hopes for the Yahoo store, but for now, he knows real success there is probably still years off.

"If I could give sellers any advice," Johns says, "it is to hang in there. Do whatever it takes to succeed. Getting the consultant was the hardest thing I ever did because up until that point I'd done it all myself. But, without them, I don't think I'd be here today.

"Don't be afraid to seek out help," John said. "It saved my business.

Jim – Part Time eBayer

Jim calls himself a junker.

"For thirty-five years," he says, "I've gone to every auction and estate sale I can. I always seemed to walk away with several boxes of stuff, books, magazines, bric-a-brac, car parts, just about anything you can think of really.

"At the same time, I am one of those guys you see picking through your neighbor's trash; you know when they set out the furniture and everything after they've cleaned out the attic or the garage. It's amazing the kind of things they throw away! I've got computers, printers, TV's, VCR's, even twenty or thirty dollars in cans several times.

"By 2009, I'd filled two garages and a couple of sheds with all this stuff. I think I'm one of those guys Frank and Mike from *American Pickers* would love to come across. My collection includes old toys, milk bottles, bikes, you name it, spread out everywhere.

"My wife passed away a few years ago. It got me to thinking what would happen to all this stuff if I wasn't here? I didn't want to stick the kids with having to get rid of it all.

"A neighbor told me about *Craigslist*. I sold some of the furniture and TV's on there. It was easy enough. I took a few pictures, wrote a couple of lines about what I had, and put it out there. I got a lot of calls, and I made somewhere around $500 that first week and a half.

"That got me thinking about eBay. I'd purchased a few things there over the years. I figured it might be time to start selling some things, too.

"The first thing I sold was an old pedal car from the 1940's. It was well used and just starting to get some rust spots. Thirty-three people bid on it, and it sold for $427.00. I paid twenty bucks for it back in the early sixties."

Jim told me, "That sale got me excited about selling on eBay."

He went on to describe a lot of his better sales. There were a lot of old toys, some silver dollars, and a lot of smaller things that went for just a few dollars. "Of course," Jim added, "there were also a lot of disappointments. Some things wouldn't sell no matter how much I lowered the price. Others, I thought would sell for a whole lot, might just as well have not sold.

"But, overall," he said, "I enjoy selling on eBay, and I make some good money, too. I also get the chance to meet a lot of interesting people. Many of them email to compliment me on the items I sell or tell me about something similar they had when they were growing up.

"Other times, when I wasn't sure what it was that I was selling, someone would email me and tell me what it was, or that I spelled the name wrong. Every time they gave me more details" he said, "I'd update my listing, and many times I'd get more bids because now I had it listed correctly."

Jim is seventy-three now. He still enjoys selling on eBay, although he has started to slow down the number of items he lists. He has a few hundred items in his eBay store and adds fifteen or twenty items per week.

Sarah – eBay Educational Specialist

Sarah got her start on eBay like a lot of people, buying stuff. She enjoys reading history and science fiction, and eBay offered her an unending supply of new books. Her first year on eBay Sarah probably bought seventy-five books. She also found herself buying DVD's for the kids, and occasionally some clothes.

The selling bug caught her late in 2006. After completing her one hundredth eBay transaction, she told herself, "Why not give selling a shot?"

At first, she sold back some of the books she had originally bought on eBay. Another time she cleaned out the garage and decided that rather than making her yearly garage sale, she would sell those items on eBay. Sarah says, "That sale netted me $327.12. My friends didn't believe me when I told them what I made, but pretty soon, several of them asked me if I could sell a few items for them, too."

She sold an electric guitar for one friend and got a whopping $1225.00. Another time, she sold a cameo and some old jewelry for $373.00. After that everyone in the neighborhood asked her to sell something for them, or asked her for advice on how they could become eBay sellers, too.

Over a six-month period, Sarah helped three of her friends start to sell on eBay. She spent more time helping friends learn how to sell. Sarah enjoyed teaching people how to sell. To do a better job, she read every book she could get her hands on about how to sell on eBay.

In early 2009 she learned about eBay University and the eBay Educational Specialists program. That intrigued her. Sarah spent some time exploring the program. She talked to some of the instructors listed in the directory and was lucky enough to find a lady who lived close to her who was willing to sit down with her and answer a lot of the questions she had about the program. Sarah took one of the classes a few weeks later. That sold her on the program.

What Sarah liked about the Educational Specialists Program was it provided her with a structured way to present information to her students. Another plus was the fact she was provided with a PowerPoint presentation to supplement the information she gave in her classes, and there was an optional workbook she could provide students to help them learn.

She's been teaching classes for four years now and says she learns as much from the students as they do from her. "It always surprises me," says Sarah. "They have some great ideas about what to sell. Most of them are always so excited to get started."

One of the things she enjoys is working with seniors. "Many of them are still coming to grips with how to use a computer, but that doesn't stop them from wanting to learn more about how they can buy and sell stuff on eBay.

"I had this one lady several years ago," she said. "She was so excited to learn how to sell because she wanted to make some extra money to help her granddaughter pay her way through college. And, I was just so touched because here's this sixty-three-year-old grandmother who'd never used a computer until three months ago. Now she wanted to make some money at it for such a great cause."

"I've probably helped several dozen moms over the years who've wanted to break away from their jobs so they could stay home with their kids while they were growing up."

"Because of eBay," she continued, "I'm doing what I always wanted to do - Helping people!"

Barb – eBay Newbie

Barb is a newbie.

By day, Barb is an assistant manager at a woman's clothing store. She hopes to become a manager in the next twelve to eighteen months. Because she's new on the job, money is a little tight right now. She hopes that she can make a consistent $500.00 per month on eBay so she can buy a new car.

Last month, she made $225.00 on $500.00 in sales, so she's about half way there.

She's only been selling on eBay for about two months and is still trying to figure the whole thing out. She's got about fifty sales under her belt now.

Most of her sales have been women's and children's clothes she picked up at *Good Will* and other thrift stores. She's familiar with fashion because of her job, so Barb knows what brands and styles are in demand. She's thinking of buying a lot of the closeouts where she works and trying her luck selling them, but she's afraid it might create a conflict of interest if anyone finds out.

Last week, she picked up some good deals at *T. J. Maxx* and *Kohl's* and is hoping to make some real money there.

How to price the items she sells is one of Barb's biggest concerns. Up until now, she has been starting all her auctions out at double what she paid for them.

The problem is quite a few of her items get snapped up within a few hours of listing them by people who use the buy-it-now option. Another forty percent of her items don't sell at all, even when she lowers the price.

Last week, Barb tweaked some of her prices. She picked out seven things she thought would sell well and decided to start the bidding at four times what she paid. Five items sold with buy-it-now, even with the higher prices. One sold at the starting price, and the other one didn't get any bids at all.

Barb was pretty excited with the results of her pricing experiment. She is going to continue stretching her prices and see what happens.

Another thing that worries Barb is what to do with her unsold items. She can't afford to keep relisting them as auctions because of the fees, but she's not sure that she's ready for an eBay store, either.

For now, Barb plans to keep selling everything at auction, while she does a little more research on eBay stores. She wants to make sure it's the right move for her.

Davis – High School Student

Davis is still a senior in high school. No one would know that by looking at his eBay store.

He has been selling on eBay for just over nine months. After three months, he opened an eBay store. He used some of his profits and had a professional designer layout his eBay store and selling template.

He wants me to stress he's not a millionaire – YET!

Right now, he makes about a thousand dollars a month, and he's okay with that. He bought a 2002 Mustang convertible last week, with cash. "How many high school seniors can say that?"

He sells Manga and Anime. And, business is booming.

"I started out by selling some of the books in my collection," says Davis. "I've got over 1200 books in my collection, and it's still growing. I've also got 63 DVD's – *Death Note*, *Yugioh*, *Bleach*, *Naruto*, and more.

"The way I got started was, I wanted to get *The Walking Dead Collection*, and I didn't have sixty bucks, so

I got mom to let me sell some stuff on her eBay account. Before I knew it, I had a hundred dollars the first week, and I had close to that again the next week.

"After four weeks of this I talked mom into letting me open an eBay account, and the first thing I did was open an eBay store.

"In two weeks, I had two hundred books and twenty-five DVDs for sale in my eBay store. After that, I talked with some of my friends about what I was doing. A lot of them sold me some of the stuff they didn't want any more. A few of them just gave me the things, and said 'Good Luck!'

"It's been a lot of fun," said Davis, "and one of the reasons I think my items sell so well is I know my stuff. I've read most of these series. Unlike a lot of the bigger sellers, I don't just go with the catalog description. I write my reviews and try to tell people how cool the stories and characters are. I don't give any spoilers or anything like that, but I let people know I'm excited, and I'm sure they will be too, if they read the books, or watch the DVDs.

"How cool is that! I get to work with the stuff I love, and I can read all of the books before I mail them."

Davis plans on dominating eBay's Manga and Anime categories before he graduates from high school. He's already set his sights on Amazon, and his website.

Terry – Automobile Internet Manager

Terry has been the Internet Manager at a small-town Chevy dealership for nearly ten years.

Most of his job involves responding to customer emails about cars listed on the dealer's website and calling potential clients to book appointments for the salesmen. Occasionally, he posts some banners on the website or fills in as a salesman if they are short of people.

Several of the salesmen have posted autos on eBay for the dealership over the years. Most of the cars they listed were fixer uppers that would have been sold at auction otherwise. Because the cars were fixer uppers, many of them had rust or mechanical problems that didn't get described correctly. As a result, the dealership had ten sales with a 2.5 overall feedback rating.

In 2011 the dealership got a new sales manager. The dealership he came from had a significant presence on eBay. One of the new responsibilities he assigned Terry was to post the dealership's inventory on the site.

Other than buying a few movies now and then, Terry had no idea how eBay worked. One of the first things he did was call customer service at eBay to ask for some pointers. They gave him some good advice and suggested a few places he could go for help.

Terry called the internet manager at his sales manager's old dealership and received several great ideas to help him get started.

Terry decided to open a new eBay account in the dealership's name. He didn't want to battle bad feedback when he was just starting out.

They had some options starting out. Several of the providers he found had the ability to post their entire inventory on eBay and Craigslist. The dealership decided they didn't want to try that especially when they were just getting started with eBay. The costs would have been over $2000 per month between their eBay store fees and the service provider's charges.

Management was also unsure whether they wanted to put their new car selection on eBay. The thought was they would have had to show significant discounts to generate any interest there.

The final decision was to start out slow and only list special cars on eBay. The first week Terry listed a 1978 El Camino, a 1982 Trans Am, and an old Ford four-wheel drive pickup.

Of the three, the Ford pickup was the only one to sell.

As the dealership listed and sold more cars on eBay, it refined its strategy. They got a better idea about what type of cars would sell to eBay customers, and which ones they should steer clear of listing on the site.

Two years later, they've sold fifty-seven cars on eBay. In that same time, they listed one hundred and fifty-two cars, so they sell about one-third of the cars they list.

They also worked out a great system for choosing which cars to list on eBay. Right off, they decided against trying to sell any auction block specials. Time has shown them that the best cars to sell on eBay are something special or unique. Old sports cars sell very well in any condition. The same goes for just about any type of four-wheel drive pickups in the $6000 to $10,000 price range. They've also had some good luck with luxury cars, and have sold a few Porsche's, Infinity's, and a Lexus, or two.

Terry sold two boats, a "big ass" RV, and several motorcycles the dealership took in trade.

Going forward, they want to expand their eBay sales and are watching the papers and local auctions for cars they think would be a good fit for their business.

Terry says he would recommend eBay for any dealership. "It's a great way to increase sales, but it also means you need to be prepared to work with online customers. We are in Iowa. Many of our clients come from Minnesota, Wisconsin, Missouri, and even as far away as California or New York.

"You need to coordinate financing and titling for them. And, because many of our customers are flying in just to pick up a new car, you need to be sure everything is ready for them when they get there. One time we sold a Nissan 370 Z to a guy from Canada. The paperwork dragged out for weeks. Finally, we told them it was ready. They had their driver on the way to pick it up when we discovered we needed another paper. We got it taken care of at the last minute with Fed Ex, but it could have caused some problems because of the distance they had to travel.

"My advice is to take every sale you can. But make sure everyone is on board before you get started. You need the cooperation of finance, management, sales people, and your titling department. Everyone has to be willing to work together."

Read These Books Next

eBay for Dummies by Marsha Collier. (Like all of the Dummies books, this one is a fun, easy read, and gives you a lot of great info to boot. You will find this especially helpful if you're new to eBay selling.

eBay 101: Selling on eBay for Part-time or Full-time Income by Steve Weber. Weber has written books about how to sell on all of the major online markets, eBay, Amazon, and Etsy. Another of his books, Barcode Booty, will show you how you can find items to sell in retail stores, thrift shops, library sales, and more, simply by using your cell phone and a barcode scanner.

eBay Power Seller Secrets: Insider Tips Form eBays Most Successful Sellers by Brad Schepp and Debra Schepp. This book helped me a lot back when I first started selling on eBay. A lot of the information is dated now, but you should still be able to pick up some useful tips.

Good Sellers, Bad Buyers: Protecting Yourself on eBay by Lexie Thornton. I just picked this book up during a free promotion last week. Learn how to protect yourself in everything you do on eBay from writing descriptions to shipping. I would strongly recommend this book.

eBay Photography the Smart Way by Joseph T. Sinclair and Stanley Livingston. This book will help you nail photographing any type of item for eBay. If you want to sell more items, better pictures are a sure way to draw more bidders.

How to Start and Run an eBay Consignment Business by Skip McGrath. This book is from 2006 so some of the information is going to be outdated, but if you are interested in selling items for other people, you can learn a lot from this book.

Easy HTML for eBay by Nicholas Chase. One thing that can help every eBay seller spruce up their listings is a basic understanding of html (the computer language used to build web pages). Another bonus is it's available for just one penny on Amazon.

Turn eBay Data Into Dollars by Ina Steiner. Ina Steiner, (a co-founder of the *eComerce Bytes Blog*) scored a homerun with this book. Once again, I have to tell you that some of the information provided is dated, but if you really want to understand how to apply data to auction pricing and selling, this is the best book available on the subject.

Tax Loopholes For eBay Sellers: Pay Less Tax and Make More Money by Diane Kennedy and Janelle Elms. Tax laws have changed since this book was published but it will give you a lot of ideas you probably never thought of about how your part time eBay business can help you save big money on taxes.

Bonus Excerpt

(If you've ever thought of selling services online, Fiverr is hands down the easiest site to get started using. Tens of thousands of people have discovered Fiverr is a great way to make it big, five bucks at a time. These are the first two chapters of my book, **Fiverr MBA: Join the GIG Economy. Make More Money, Enjoy More Freedom**.

The Very Least You Need to Know

Fiverr is relatively new to the e-commerce scene. Micha Kaufman and Shai Wininger founded the company in 2010. All gigs start at $5.00, but that's changing as the site continues to reinvent itself. Sellers receive $4.00 for each completed gig. Fiverr's take is twenty percent or $1.00 from each five-dollar gig.

As of October 2016, there were over three million gigs listed on Fiverr. The bad news is that over one million of those gigs didn't receive a bite—not one. If that's not a good reason to read this book, I don't know what is.

Fiverr has a leveling system, like eBay's Top-Rated Seller Program.

- **Newbies** have limited options on Fiverr. They can offer two gig extras limited to $5.00, $10.00, and $20.00. New sellers are limited to accepting four gigs in one transaction.

- **Level One** status opens up more opportunities for sellers. To reach Level One status, Fiverr's need to complete ten gigs in the previous thirty days with a minimum 90% satisfaction rating. After they level up, sellers can list up to 15 gigs at a time, offer "fast delivery" for extra profits, and provide custom orders up to $1500. Level One status also opens up another gig extra—for a total of three, and allows sellers to accept eight orders in one transaction.

- **Level Two Sellers** are required to have completed 50 gigs in the last sixty days with a minimum 90% satisfaction rating. When they reach this level, sellers can increase their income significantly. Buyers can purchase up to twelve of their gigs at one time. Gig Extras jump to five, and the price range increases to $5.00, $10.00, $20.00, and $40,00.

- Becoming a **Top-Rated Seller** is like receiving tenure at a major university. The process for reaching this status is somewhat mysterious. The Fiverr blog states **the site editors "mutually" choose top Rated Sellers**. What is clear though is once you receive this designation a whole new world of profit possibilities open up to you. **Top-rated Sellers** can charge up to $100 for each gig extra, and they receive the **Top-Rated Seller** Badge next to each of their gigs.

If you're serious about making money on Fiverr, you need to level up as quickly as possible. The easiest way to do this is to offer a variety of gigs and provide excellent customer service.

Jon says it took him "a week to move from **Newbie** to **Level One**. In another thirty days, I had my **Level Two** badge. From my very first day on Fiverr, the orders kept pouring in. And, do you want to know why? Because all of my gigs offered great value, people spent their money with me.

"I didn't worry about how much money I was making, or how long it took to do the job. The *Golden Ticket* I was shooting for was *five-star feedback*. Three months after I started on Fiverr, I had a perfect feedback rating on 257 sales.

"That's worth more than any amount of money I could have made at that time. It opened up bigger gig extras, larger dollar sales, and, did I mention—less than two years later, Fiverr selected me as a **Top-Rated Seller**."

Custom Offers Will Take Your Business to a New Level

What would you think if I told you, you could quadruple or quintuple your Fiverr income by doing just one thing?

Would you be interested?

And, what if I told you, it wouldn't take much more effort than you are investing right now. Would you be interested?

Of course, you would, right?

What I'm talking about is Fiverr's new *Custom Offer* feature. It's this nifty new tool that lets you create custom packages targeted towards a buyer's individual wants and needs.

Not too long ago *Forbes Magazine* published an article about an executive resume writer who took her income from several thousand dollars per month to thirty thousand dollars per month. By sending highly targeted *Custom Offers* to business executives, she increased her average gig revenue to $800.

Not bad, for writing a resume.

Another seller on Fiverr's website said he talked to a client about making money online, and the next thing he knew he was sending them a *Custom Offer* to give a personalized presentation to their customers.

How cool is that?

What baffles me, though, is when I receive *Custom Offers* from sellers who think small.

Last week I received *Custom Offers* from two sellers who offered me a book promotion gig. They promised to promote my book to what seemed like six bazillion people for just $5.00.

That doesn't even make sense.

If they went to all the bother to search completed gigs on Fiverr to find potential customers, why would they make such a wimpy offer?

Book promotions go for big bucks.

Many times, I've spent $400 or $500 on a single book campaign. The larger websites like BookBub charge upwards of $250. FreeBooksy costs $75 or higher, and BargainBooksy starts at $25.

If the person making the *Custom Offer* knows their business, they should know what similar companies are charging. If that's the case, why are they offering a five dollar service when they could easily charge $25 or $100?

It's an example of what I would call the think small and grovel syndrome.

Honestly, *Custom Offers* are a great way to boost your income, but to take advantage of them, you've got to think big. You need to understand your category, your customer's pain points, and how your services can help customers relieve their pain and suffering.

Think of yourself as a doctor.

If you copyedit and proofread manuscripts, you need to look at the big-picture. Instead of just editing for spelling and grammar errors, what other services would benefit your customers?

Could you analyze their documents and ensure they are following the correct stylesheet? Could you annotate their manuscript and let them know if they failed to introduce a new character? Or, maybe you could let them know they forgot to footnote a quote or fact?

Sometimes, a writer just needs another unbiased eye on his manuscript to tell him (or her) what works, or what doesn't work and why. Sometimes, an extra set of eyes on a manuscript can make all the difference.

Every time you receive an order or inquiry, you could follow up with a *Custom Offer* that details what other services you offer. Maybe, you only receive one order for every ten or fifteen *Custom Offers* you send out but say it brings in an extra $250 in revenue.

Is it worth it? Would it change your business? Would it change your lifestyle?

So, what's the best way to get started using *Custom Offers*?

First off, sellers need to understand Fiverr limits how many *Custom Offers* you can send each day. *Level One* sellers can send three offers a day; *Level Two* sellers can send ten.

Other than that, there are several ways to get started.

1. Some sellers send them to everyone who places a new order. The best way to do this is to look at what your customer ordered, the buyer's previous order history on Fiverr, and then think about how

you can add value. If the purchaser is an author, visit their Amazon author page. Do they have Kindle, paperback, and audiobooks for each of their titles? Send them a *Custom Offer* for all three. It might not work, but with just a little more effort on your part, it gives you a chance to triple your income in each order.

2. A lot of buyers troll the gig request list. When they find one they can do, they shoot off a *Custom Offer*. The advantage here is if you're a new seller, not having feedback isn't a problem. Buyers can't see your ranking, so it doesn't work against you when you send a *Custom Offer*. The only thing I would advise is not to link to one of your gigs, instead, tailor a deal for each offer. And, for God's sake, charge more than $5.00. You're worth it.

3. Use *Fiverr Anywhere* to post deals on your website, blog, social media sites, and in targeted email campaigns. Doing this gives you the best chance to get your offer out there to anyone who may benefit from it.

Example 1.

> Hi, I'm Jill from the US. I'm working on facebook and other social medias with promotion campaigns. I can help you to promote your kindle book in facebook. In this offer, I will do my "Large page promotion" extra for free with my basic gig. Also I'm giving extra fast delivery for free!!This is a good offer, and it is for limited period. Please order my gig. Hope to give you the best result. Thank you!

It's obvious; this seller should have given this *Custom Offer* some more thought before sending it out. The misspellings and grammatical mistakes make it apparent the offer isn't worth the five dollars the seller is asking.

A better proposal would read something like this.

> Hi, I'm Jill from the United States. I'm an expert in Facebook, Twitter, and Pinterest marketing, and can help promote your Kindle eBook. I've been helping author's launch new books for over five years now, and have played an integral part in moving over fifty titles to number one in their category. While I can't make any promises, I

guarantee I will do my best to get your book moving up the charts.

Do you see the difference?

It's well written, engaging, and everything in it works to position the seller as an expert in book marketing. The first Custom Offer would have had a hard time getting anyone to spend five dollars; the second one could easily have asked for fifty to one hundred dollars because it built value into it.

Example 2.

Hi, I'm John, and I've been a resume writer on Fiverr for over six months now. No matter what industry you're searching in, I can write the perfect resume. Need a new cover letter? I can help with that, too.

Not bad. But not good, either.

What do you think of this one?

Good Morning. My name is John. I've worked as a career counselor and resume specialist for the last twenty-five years. I ensure high-level executives in the telecommunications field make the best first impression with their resumes and cover letters. I do things a little different than most sellers on Fiverr. I get to know you, your goals, and what you want to accomplish before I start working. That way you get a resume and cover letter tailored to your career goals. It's a different style of doing business on Fiverr, but the results speak for themselves. My feedback is impeccable, but if you have any questions or concerns, I'd be happy to address them before we get started.

What do you think?

Would you buy from John? Of course, you would, because he's the real deal. In less than 100 words, he positioned himself as an industry expert, and the guy you would want to have on your side in any job search campaign.

If you want to take your custom offers to the next level—tailor them to your customer's wants, needs, and desires. You will hit more home runs when you do it this way.

www.ingramcontent.com/pod-product-compliance
Lightning Source LLC
Chambersburg PA
CBHW020920180526
45163CB00007B/2822